Leaflookers' Guide to
Splendor in the Mountains

Text by: John W. Powell

Photography &
Photography Tips by: Moody Barrick

Mountain Splendor Publications, Inc.

Printing by Pacific Printing Press, Inc.
Orlando, Florida

i

ACKNOWLEDGMENTS

Our appreciation to Sue Powell for typing, editing and all the "details" related to manuscript preparation. Also, a word of thanks to Michael and Susan B of Pacific Printing Press, Inc. for their helpful suggestions and patience in preparing the manuscript and photos for print.

And to "mother nature", for creating such a spectacle which compels some of us to become excited enough to attempt to put into words and pictures a visual image which can never do justice to the "real thing", goes our deep appreciation and respect.

Contents

1

FORWARD
SPLENDOR IN THE MOUNTAINS

This book is dedicated to all those people, both natives and tourists, who are fortunate enough to witness the "Splendor in the Mountains" which occurs each autumn in north Georgia, western North Carolina and southeastern Tennessee.

Words and pictures, no matter how expressive, cannot begin to describe the beauty of the actual visual spectacle. It is hoped that this book can add to the enjoyment we all experience during this very special time.

Photo F-1: Color reflections. Mirror Lake, Highlands, North Carolina.

INTRODUCTION

The Blue Ridge Mountain range originates in southern Pennsylvania and extends 615 miles into northern Georgia. At their widest, they extend east to west for 70 miles in North Carolina. The height, in most of the range, varies from 2,000 feet to 4,000 feet. However, it is not uncommon for many peaks to exceed 5,000 feet and some even 6,000 feet.

The Blue Ridge Mountain range constitutes one of the major recreation areas of the south. The waterfalls, the hiking trails and the sheer beauty of the mountains, serve the recreational pursuits of millions of people yearly. The fall colors alone draw hundreds of thousands of tourists each year. As evidenced by the picture on the preceding page (Photo F-1), few visual scenes can be as overwhelming and beautiful as the autumn colors in the mountains. The Blue Ridge Mountains contain a wide variety of colorful trees and weather conditions which produce peak colors, second to none.

The Great Smoky Mountains make up the other dominant range which forms the Appalachian chain. These famous, beautiful mountains contain ideal conditions for tree and wildlife growth. In addition to an impressive variety of trees, this range also boasts many record size species. Trees flourish in this area.

One thing which makes fall such an exciting time in the mountains is that during October there will be peak color at some location. A minimum amount of travel can produce a "leaf lookers" delight. In a good year, fall colors may last well into the month of November.

Enjoy your visit to our mountain spectacle and it is hoped that this book will add to your enjoyment and appreciation for one of the miracles of mother nature.

Photo 1: Graveyard Fields - Mile Marker #418 Blue Ridge Parkway

CHAPTER I
THE PROCESS OF COLOR CHANGE

What Causes This Beauty?

The beauty which surrounds us during the autumn color season represents the coming together of many of mother nature's schemes. The process of color change can be scientifically validated but is still not very well understood. Even those people who have lived in the mountains all their lives, still base much of their knowledge on conjecture and beliefs handed down through generations of families. What probably leads to this confusion is the fact that all color seasons are spectacular. Regardless of conditions, the beauty of the fall somehow manages to emerge. It's just that some seasons are more spectacular than others. Let's examine the why.

WEATHER: The fall color season is controlled totally by weather conditions, although not in the manner that many people think. For example, many believe that an early frost is needed in order to enhance the brightness of the colors. In actuality, an early freeze can dull the colors tremendously by killing or damaging the leaves. The intensity of colors will be greatly reduced by an early frost.

The bright red colors can form only in certain leaves and results from large amounts of stored sugar. This sugar storage is enhanced by cool weather and bright sunshine. Hence, you have two of the needed weather conditions to promote a vivid color season: bright sunshine and cool weather. It is ironic that leaves reach their peak of beauty shortly before dying and being shed. This shedding process is necessary in order for the tree to live through the cold weather. The tree trunk and limbs need all the available water so the leaves are shed for this reason. Meanwhile, mother nature allows us the privilege of enjoying the buds, the flowering, and in some cases, the colorful berries of the leaf's life cycle. To only notice trees and leaves during the fall season, is to miss out on incredible beauty during the other seasons.

Weather conditions which tend to inhibit the color changing process include a hard frost, an early snow, excessive rainfall and strong winds. On the other hand, a warm cloudy fall will also tend to reduce the vivid colors. In light of these negative weather conditions, let's now examine the ideal weather conditions for producing a spectacular color season...... Bright sunshiny days with cool evenings, approaching, but not reaching freezing temperatures and a minimum amount of rainfall and lack of strong, gusty winds, is ideal.

Remember, there is no bad color season, only some which are better than others. Even in off years, the color change produces a beautiful spectacle.

The three pictures, shown below and on the following page (Photos 1-1, 1-2 and 1-3) present a graphic illustration of several factors involved in color change. These three pictures were taken of the same red maple at three stages of color change. The tree is located in Sky Valley, Georgia. Picture one was taken on October 15th, picture two: October 19th, picture three: October 28th. The 3rd picture represents the peak color of this particular tree.

It is interesting to note not only the three stages of color but also the order of the color change. Note that in picture one, the color appears to be going from yellow to red. In picture three, the dominant color is orange. In other words, in this particular tree the color went from yellow to red to orange. This only serves to demonstrate that each tree of the same species can turn a different color and individual leaves on a tree can also go through a different color changing process.

Photo 1-1: (Picture #1) October 15th, 1st stage of change.

10

Photo 1-2: (Picture #2) October 19th, 2nd stage of change.

Photo 1-3: (Picture #3) October 28th, 3rd stage of change.

11

Photosynthesis

Photosynthesis, as we all learned in biology class, is the process which causes leaves to turn green. Chlorophyll is the actual ingredient which causes the green. As winter approaches, the tree shuts off the nutrients which are necessary for this process. As this chlorophyll is used up, the green begins to fade and other colors emerge.

The picture below (Photo 1-4) graphically illustrates this process. The red color will slowly begin to dominate until the entire leaf is red.

Photo 1-4: Photosynthesis in process - Maple leaf.

Photo 1-5: Photosynthesis affects each leaf differently.

The Reds, the Yellows and the Oranges

Now that we know why the green is phased out, lets examine the other colors which begin to dominate the leaf. As was mentioned earlier, the red colors need large amounts of stored sugar in order to be especially brilliant. These reds (anthocyanins), unlike the yellows (carotenoids), which have been present in the leaves all along, are carried in the tree sap. The green color is so intense that it covers up and hides the reds and yellows. As photosynthesis begins to shut down, the green starts to disappear and the yellows, reds and oranges begin to emerge. Peak color for a specific leaf arrives when the green is totally gone and the other colors have taken over. The yellow color is produced by the carotenoid pigment which also accounts for the yellow color of certain fruits, vegetables and flowers. These pigments produce a variety of colors that range from lemon yellow to orange. Strangely enough, these pigments also produce the yellow in butter and egg yokes since they are so persistent that even the digestive juices of animals will not break them down.

The reds or anthocyanins, range in color from pale pink through red, purple and blue. These pigments cause the brilliant red coloring in apples and many flowers. Peak color in the fall is usually characterized by the dominant bright reds. The two pictures, on the facing page (Photos 1-6 & 1-7), demonstrate the various stages of color change in the sassafras and maple leaves.

Photo 1-6: Sassafras leaves.

Photo 1-7: Maple leaves.

Timing is Everything: A peek at the Peak

The most asked question in the mountains during the fall is "when will the peak arrive?" Everyone has a theory of selecting the time but there is no fool-proof method of picking this "magic" time. However, there are several indicators or hints to guide one to an educated guess. First, one must realize that it is always a peak somewhere in the mountains during a 4 or 5 week period which encompasses the month of October and often early November. The time to travel and the willingness to do so would allow the lucky people to enjoy 4 to 5 weeks of magnificent color within the geographical region discussed in this book (See Appendix A: Map).

Obviously, the higher elevations will begin to show color first. The color starts at the very top and moves slowly down the mountainside. In extremely high elevations, some change is evident as early as mid-August, when the leaves of the Witch Hobble begin turning yellow and red. In September, the reds of the Pin Cherry and the yellow of the Birch and Mountain Ash start making their appearance.

The bright reds of the Dogwood, Sourwood and Sumac begin to show up in early September and join other early changers such as the Buckeyes (yellow), Blackgum (red) and the Hickories (yellow).

Photo 1-8: Blackgum - an early turner

Photo 1-9: Maple - a middle turner

Photo 1-10: Beech - a late turner

Listed below are examples of when certain trees "normally" produce fall color:

Early turners:	Willow (yellow) Ash (yellow) Locust (yellow) Blackgum (red)
Middle turners:	Maple (red, yellow & orange) Sassafras (orange) Cherry (red)
Late turners:	White Ash (yellow) Beech (bronze) Oak (dark brown)

In the Blue Ridge and Smoky Mountain ranges, soil conditions, weather conditions and altitude, all combine to produce a mixture of colors which are magnificant.

The Hickories, Catalpas, Sycamores, Poplars and Yellow Oaks may turn a rusty green or a pure yellow. The Black Walnuts, Redbuds, Shadbush and Mulberries are bright golden yellow. The Tulip trees offer a stark contrast of gold against the dark green of the White Pine.

Many oaks show brown colors but some turn purple, reddish brown or bronze in beautiful combinations. However, the primary color producers - Dogwoods, Sourwoods, Sourgums, Sassafras and Red Maples - are more plentiful in the south than in any other section of the country. These trees are the primary determinants of the timing of the "peak".

Photo 1-11: A peak color scene

CHAPTER II

THE MAJOR COLOR PRODUCING TREES

"I think that I shall never see......."

Joyce Kilmer wrote these introductory words to a beautiful poem many years ago. The poem, "Trees", became a classic and has been enjoyed by millions of people over the years. Who would have thought that something which appears so simple as a tree could have become so important in the lives of so many? There is a magical quality connected with trees which attracts our interest and whets our appetite for a return to nature.

The Blue Ridge and Great Smoky Mountain regions contain a wide variety of trees and ground cover which, together, form the beautiful fall foliage season. The deciduous trees (those that lose their leaves) are complimented by a wide variety of conifers, or needle bearing trees. Since these evergreen trees maintain a green appearance year round, the beautiful greens mix with the various fall colors to form a beautiful spectacle which we call the fall color season. Nowhere, in this United States, is there a more spectacular show of colors than in the north Georgia, western North Carolina and southeastern Tennessee region.

The information contained in this chapter includes both visual and factual data concerning the trees and leaves most common to the geographical area covered in this book. The map designated as Appendix A will give the reader a general idea of the region discussed in this book.

There has been no attempt to include all the trees of the area but only those which are major contributors to the color scene. Likewise, ground cover and wildflowers are not included in this book even though they contribute a great deal to the overall color scheme. Many wildflower books are available.

TULIP POPLAR
Liriodendron tulipifera

Although known as the Yellow Poplar, this tree is not related to the Poplar at all. It is, in fact, a member of the Magnolia family.

The tree appears to have taken the place of the blight infected American Chestnut and grows commonly in "stands" where chestnuts once grew. The tree is very tall and straight and forms a beautiful golden contrast of the surrounding pines. The tree is a "middle turner."

The leaf of this tree has a very distinctive shape. They are 3-6 inches long and are shaped like a saddle with four paired lobes on a long stalk.

The tree gets its name from the beautiful blossoms which open in late April or May and have a striking resemblance to tulips. These blossoms become a necessary nectar source for the bees.

This tree exists only in the United States and Western China.

Photo 2-1: Tulip leaf in fall color

Photo 2-2: Tulip Poplar

BLACKGUM
Nyssa Sylvatica

The beautiful deep scarlet colors of the Blackgum are among the first of the "early turners." This tree, which is also known as the Sourgum or Black Tupelo, is actually a member of the Dogwood family. It is not related to the Sweetgum even though both are common in the south.

The Blackgum is a medium sized tree (30-40 feet high) and actually becomes smaller with age. The top branches begin to break and fall causing decay from the top down. The diameter of the trunk is usually from 1-2 feet and the leaves are 2-6 inches long and oval shaped. The leaves are a beautiful dark green in the summer and turn to a deep crimson during the fall foliage season.

Photo 2-3: Blackgum leaf changing to red

24

Photo 2-4: Blackgum tree

SWEETGUM
Liquidambar styraciflua

The star-shaped leaves make the Sweetgum easily identifiable. The fall color of these leaves can run the gamut from bright red to a clear yellow. This stately tree may grow to heights exceeding 100 feet. The heavy, close-grained wood is highly desirable for use in furniture making and for veneered wood such as plywood. The tree gets its name from the "amber" or sweet gum which oozes from the tree. It is sometimes used for gum and is often used in the manufacture of incense and perfume. The Sweetgum is a distinctly southern tree and is a member of the Witch Hazel family.

Photo 2-5: Sweetgum leaf

Photo 2-6: Sweetgum in change

SOURWOOD
Oxydendrum arboreum

Sourwood honey, a highly desirable southern delicacy, is a product of the Sourwood. This tree, which is related to the Rhododendron and the Mountain Laurel, becomes a beautiful scarlet during the foliage season. The Sourwood is a small tree rarely growing higher than forty feet with a trunk diameter of 8-12 inches. The alternate leaves are a beautiful green in the summer. The leaves are 2-5 inches long and sparsely toothed at the margin. The leaves are unusual in that the veins are very lateral and some join the midline at almost a right angle.

The Sourwood is an early changer, with the leaves beginning to change color in late August and continuing until late October. The green fruits form a colorful contrast to the red fall colors. The tree gets its name from the acidic taste of the leaves and twigs.

Photo 2-7: Sourwood leaf in change

28

Photo 2-8: Sourwood tree

AMERICAN BEECH
Fagus Grandifolia

The American Beech is also known as the "initial tree." The tree's smooth, gray bark (see Photo 2-9) has long been used by lovers and others to carve special messages. Even messages of historical significance have been inscribed on the bark of these trees.

The tree is large, growing to well over 100 feet in some instances. The wood of the tree is close grained and water resistant, which has made it a favorite for thousands of years for the making of bowls. It is also used for flooring and furniture and is an excellent fuel wood.

The leaves are alternate and oval shaped and have long pointed tips and course, toothed margins. In the fall, the leaves turn a clear, golden yellow and then, later, a coppery bronze.

A unique feature of this tree is that many of the younger trees maintain their leaves throughout the winter. Even though these leaves have lost their fall colors and are now brown, they still add a touch of color to the otherwise colorless winter scene. The kernels of the beechnuts provide much of the winter food supply for many forest animals.

Photo 2-9: Beech leaves in mid-change

Photo 2-10: American Beech tree

Photo 2-11: The distinctive smooth bark of the Beech tree

YELLOW BIRCH
Betula Lutea Michx

The Yellow Birch, which is basically a northern or mountain tree, is distinguishable by its yellow or silvery bark. The bark has an unattractive ragged look and tends to peel off by sheets. The tree is large, often attaining heights of 100 feet or more. The wood is among the more valuable of the birches. It is heavy and close grained and is used in furniture and flooring and other items requiring strength. It is an excellent fuel wood and the bark peelings are highly flammable and are often used for starting fires. The bark of the tree is also eaten by many species of forest animals.

The leaves are nearly oval and double-toothed and ending in a sharp point. The leaves turn a golden yellow in the fall.

Photo 2-12: The Birch leaf contains toothed edges and sharp points

Photo 2-13: The golden-yellow Birch tree

Photo 2-14: The ragged and peeling bark of the Yellow Birch

33

THE MAPLES

The Maples comprise one of our most valuable species of trees. There are up to 70 kinds of maples in the world, of which, 13 types exist in the United States. The buds, twigs and the leaves of the maple are arranged in the opposite rather than the alternate plan. The Maples are beautifully shaped trees whose foliage is so dense that the stalks of some leaves will lengthen and push out in order not to be deprived of sunlight. The wood products and maple sugar and maple syrup make the Maple a highly desirable commercial tree, but the wide spectrum of fall colors makes this tree synonymous with the perception of the beauty of the fall season.

MOUNTAIN MAPLE
Dwarf Maple

This small, bushy maple is plentiful in the Blue Ridge and Smoky Mountains. The leaves are usually three-lobed with small teeth. They turn a brilliant yellow or red during the fall season. These trees are common between 3,000 and 6,000 feet and account for a great deal of the beauty during the color season.

Photo 2-15: A cluster of Mountain Maple leaves

Photo 2-16: The Mountain Maple is common to this region

RED (SCARLET) MAPLE
Acer rubrum

This tree is the most spectacular color producer of the mountain region during the fall. It is very common and if we were to perceive our color producing trees as a "team" then the red maple would surely be the "superstar" of the forest.

It is not uncommon to see this tree grow to heights of more than 100 feet. It is broad at the top and has a beautiful rounded crown. The tree differs from other maples in the red coloring of the twigs and leaf stalks. The leaf of the red maple contains "V" shaped spaces between the lobes. By contrast, most other maples contain "U" shaped spaces. The leaves are normally about four inches long with five-pointed, saw-toothed lobes. However, the leaves may be much smaller and contain only three lobes.

The wood from the red maple is not strong and durable and thus has restricted commercial uses, such as, cheap furniture and crates.

The red maple is a middle to late changer and tends to dominate when in full color. Many believe the "peak color season" has arrived when the red maple is in full color. Bright crimson is the most common color but all shades of yellow and orange are also common in these trees.

Photo 2-17: The contrasting gold leaf demonstrates the color range of the Red Maple

Photo 2-18: The magnificent Scarlet (Red) Maple

STRIPED MAPLE
Acer pensylvanicum

This Maple is also known as the "Moosewood." Although it has no commercial value, this small tree adds greatly to the fall color scene. The leaves turn a clear, bright yellow in the fall and are also beautiful during the spring budding season.

The striped maple leaves are the largest of any of the Maples and are wide, finely toothed with three lobes. The shape of the leaves has also resulted in the nickname "Goosefoot Maple." The unique bark of this tree is striped and has an artificial look and serves as favorite food for many forest animals.

Photo 2-19: The Striped Maple leaf has a close resemblance to the Mountain Maple

Photo 2-20: Striped Maple tree

SILVER MAPLE
Acer saccharinum

Although more of a planted, ornamental tree than one which grows wild, the Silver Maple is relatively common in the upper mountain regions. The fall colors range from bright to dull yellow.

The tree produces beautiful large leaves which are deeply cut and lobed with "U" shape sinuses. The leaves are green above and paler below, thus giving the tree its name.

The tree has a graceful look caused by the branches which droop down and then curve upward at the tips. The tree grows rapidly and produces a soft wood used for spools and other small articles.

Photo 2-21: The distinctive shape of the Silver Maple leaf demonstrates why it is a popular ornamental tree

Photo 2-22: A Silver Maple in the early stages of color change.

SUGAR MAPLE
Acer saccharum

The Sugar Maple is a very popular tree for many reasons. Its size and fullness make it an ideal shade tree and the beautiful fall colors of deep red, orange and yellow, make the Sugar Maple a highly sought ornamental tree.

The tree is large (70 - 100 feet) and has a rounded crown with dense foliage. The leaves are 3 1/2 to 5 1/2 inches long and almost as wide. The long lobes contain widely spaced teeth along the edges. This tree is the source of maple syrup and maple sugar and the wood is used for such things as flooring, furniture and tools.

Photo 2-23: Sugar Maple leaf

Photo 2-24: Sugar Maple in orange peak

MOUNTAIN ASH
Sorbus americana

Adding to the color season within our region are three types of Ashes. The most colorful of the trees, the Mountain Ash, is not truly an Ash but a member of the rose family. It thrives on the higher slopes of the Smoky Mountains. The tree rarely grows higher than twenty feet and may resemble a shrub more than a tree.

The tree has pinnately compound leaves (many on one twig) which are opposite. They are each 1-3 inches long and each twig will contain 9-17 individual leaves. They turn red or yellow in the fall. However, the tree produces bright red berries which remain throughout the winter and add a welcome brightness of color to the winter landscape.

The other two types of Ashes (which are true ashes) common to our region are the White Ash (fraxinus americana) and the Green Ash (fraxinus pennsylvanica). The leaves of both turn either reddish purple or yellow in the fall. Both are valuable timber trees, especially valued for use in baseball bats and other sporting implements.

The White and Green Ash are much larger trees, growing to heights up to 80 feet.

Photo 2-25: The beautiful red berries of the Mountain Ash

THE OAKS

The Oaks comprise the family of trees which are probably the most historically significant. The symbol of strength and durability and the inspiration for numerous essays and poems. The Oak lives to a ripe old age and some don't even reach full size until they are three hundred years old.

Of the 275 known species of Oak, 54 are native to America with most standing in the eastern part of the United States. These 54 Oaks divide into 2 groups; the White Oak family and the Black Oak family. Each group contains distinctive features as listed below:

White Oak:

1. Rounded leaves
2. Light colored bark
3. Acorns mature in one season
4. Inside of acorn shell is smooth
5. Kernels of acorns are sweet

Black Oak:

1. Angular and bristle tipped lobes
2. The bark is dark
3. Acorns require two seasons to mature
4. Inside of acorn is hairy
5. Kernels of acorns are bitter

The following three Oaks are among the most common mountain growers and are the ones which contribute most to the fall color scene.

BLACK OAK
Quercus Velutina

The tree derives its name from the fact that as the tree gets older, the bark becomes black. It is a large massive tree with crooked, wide spreading branches. The shape of this tree fits most people's conception of what an oak should look like. The inner bark is yellow causing the tree to also be known as the Yellow Oak, and is used as a dye.

The leaves are variable in size and shape. They measure up to 10 inches long and up to 8 inches wide. The lobes are bristle tipped (as are all Black Oak family species) and broadest across the upper lobes. They become bright yellow in the fall.

The wood of this tree is typical of the oaks. Strong and durable and used mainly in construction lumber.

Photo 2-26: The unique bristle-tipped leaves of the Black Oak

CHESTNUT OAK
Quercus prinus

The Chestnut Oak is also known as the Rock Chestnut and is very abundant in the mountains. The leaves are similar to the Chestnut leaves but do not have the bristly points of their namesake. The leaves are long (5-9 inches), oblong and irregularly waved on the margin. In the fall, they turn yellow before turning to a deep yellow brown.

The wood from this tree is in demand since it is heavy, durable and holds up well in the soil. Much of the wood is used as construction lumber. The bark also produces tanner, used for the tanning of leather.

The acorn kernel of this tree is a major food producer for the gray squirrel and other animals.

Photo 2-27: The Chestnut Oak leaf turns yellow, then brown

Photo 2-28: The Chestnut Oak tree

SCARLET OAK
Quercus coccinea

Second to none in adding to the fall color explosion, this tree is among the most beautiful. The leaves turn a brilliant scarlet and as late turners are significant indicators of the elusive "peak".

The tree is among our most common and due to its fall beauty is often planted for ornamental purposes. The tree is large, growing to heights of 75 feet with randomly shaped branches.

The leaf is distinct with 7 bristle tip lobes. The leaf has deeply cut sinuses which extend almost to the mid-rib and are "U" shaped.

This tree is a member of the Black Oak family and bears small acorns which are surrounded by beautiful little cups. The acorns require two years to develop.

This is a major color producing tree in our mountainous region.

Photo 2-29: Scarlet Oak leaf

50

Photo 2-30: The contrasting blue sky brings out the beautiful color of the Scarlet Oak

HICKORIES

The word which may best describe the Hickory family is versatility. This native American tree is used in more ways than any of our trees. Like the closely related Walnut, it produces an edible fruit (nut) and an extremely valuable wood. With the Indians, the nut was a necessary food source used in a variety of ways. Although the hickory nut remains a food source, the wood from the tree has more value to modern society. The wood is exceptionally strong, and widely used for handles.

Although there are many kinds of Hickories, most are similar and all which exist, in this region, turn a bright yellow in the fall. The Hickory varieties of Mockernut, Bitternut, Shagbark and Pignut, are all discussed in this section but only the Mockernut tree and leaf are pictured. Specific descriptions are offered of the others.

The wood makes an excellent fuel and is unsurpassed for smoking and flavoring various meats.

The Hickory has held an important place in the development of our country. The old sayings, "tough as Hickory," are not without foundation. The Hickory is a tree of historical significance.

BITTERNUT HICKORY
Carya cordiformis

Because of the graceful appearance of the Bitternut, many consider it the most beautiful of the Hickories. It commonly grows to heights of 100 feet or more.

The leaves are smaller than those of other Hickories, with 7-11 leaflets, which are finely toothed. Obviously, the kernel of the nut is very bitter.

The wood of this tree is reddish brown in color and not as valuable as other hickory wood. The tree is sometimes called the "Red Hickory" because of the color of the wood.

SHAGBARK HICKORY
Carya ovata

The most popular of the Hickories is the Shagbark, mostly because of the sweetness of the nut kernel. This tree is not nearly so common to the area covered by this book.

The Shagbark is not as handsome as the other Hickories. It grows tall and straight but the crown is usually uneven and oblong. In many cases, the lower branches are shorter than the upper branches. The tree gets its name from the loose, shaggy bark of the older trees. This bark appears to be attached in the middle and is loose at each end. The younger trees have a smooth bark which does not furrow until later.

The leaves are large and compound and usually have 5 or 7 leaflets. The upper leaflets are broad and large while the pair nearest the base are much smaller. The tips are pointed and the edges are finely-toothed. The leaves turn a yellowish brown in the fall. This is not the most colorful of the Hickories.

PIGNUT HICKORY
Carya glabra

The Pignut Hickory is probably the least common to the mountainous region even though it has a wide range in the north, midwest and south. The tree is medium to large size, reaching heights of 60 feet or more. It has unusually slender branches which tend to group at the lower part of the tree. The bark of the tree is gray with a firm looking appearance. The irregular furrows form a diamond shaped pattern. The leaves are 8-12 inches long with 5-7 leaflets. They are smooth with finely serrated edges. The leaves of this Hickory are among the most colorful of the Hickories, turning a bright yellow or orange during the fall season.

Strangely enough, the nut of this tree can sometimes produce a kernel with a delicately sweet taste, but often it is very bitter. The wood of this tree is among the best of the Hickories and is used for much the same purposes as the others.

MOCKERNUT HICKORY
Carya tomentosa

The name Mockernut comes from the fact that the nuts of this tree contain very small kernels which is a disappointment to those used to reaping the benefits of the Shagbark nut. In addition to being small, the nuts are often bitter in taste.

The leaves of the tree are large, being 8-12 inches long with 7-9 oblong leaflets. The margins are fine-toothed, except near the base, where the margins become smooth. When bruised, the leaves emit a pleasing and distinctive odor. The leaves turn a beautiful yellow during the fall season.

Photo 2-31: Mockernut leaf

Photo 2-32: Mockernut Hickory tree

AMERICAN CHESTNUT
Castanea dentata

The story of the American Chestnut is a sad one and one from which we can learn something. Through no fault of our own, a valuable asset can cease to exist. We are at the mercy of mother nature and the beauty which we now enjoy should be taken full advantage of. Every effort must be made to protect our trees and other environmental treasures.

The Chestnut blight, which is believed to have come from China, has completely destroyed our Chestnut tree. No cure has been found even though the blight is now nearly a hundred years old. The tree exists now only in sprouts which all will die as they grow bigger. Strangely enough, the gold colors of the sprouts still add greatly to our fall color scene here in the mountains.

No tree was more important in the lives of our colonial settlers. The kernel of the chestnut had many edible uses and the wood of the Chestnut, although light, was water resistant and was ideal for use as fence posts and fence railing.

The leaves of the Chestnut are alternate, oblong-shaped with long, pointed tips. They are 5-7 inches long and each vein ends in a tooth.

Hopefully, a cure will be found for the blight which is killing this magnificent tree and it will be restored to its rightful place as one of the giants of our tree population.

Photo 2-33: The golden leaves of a disappearing species

Photo 2-34: A small Chestnut which has resisted the blight

SASSAFRAS
Sassafras albidum

The Sassafras tree ranges considerably in size from a small shrub to a large tree. However, in the mountainous area it is rarely seen in its taller form. This is a very versatile tree, with a colorful history of having medicinal value. Even though this thinking is gone, the Sassafras is used to flavor medicine and as a perfume for soaps. It is also interesting to note that the powdered leaves are still used in Louisiana as a flavoring and thickening for gumbo soup. Obviously, sassafras tea is the best known of the products of this tree.

The leaves of the Sassafras vary widely, some being entire and some mitton-lobed. Many have as few as one lobe and as many as four. The leaves range from yellow to bright orange during the fall season. The leaves are large, up to, and sometimes exceeding 6 inches in length and up to 4 inches wide.

The Sassafras tree is one of the most unusual, interesting and useful of all the mountain trees.

Photo 2-35: A three-lobed leaf

Photo 2-36: The versatile Sassafras tree

FLOWERING DOGWOOD
Cornus florida

Nothing is more characteristic of the south than the Flowering Dogwoods. The tree is small, rarely reaching more than 30 feet with a diameter of 6 to 12 inches. However, large trees are not uncommon. Of the 15 American species of Dogwood, the flowering variety, whether it be the native white or the cultivated pink variety, is by far the best.

The tree is small and low branching with the limbs spreading outward and downward, seemingly to emphasize the beauty of the white blooms. The Dogwood is one of the few color producing trees which is even more beautiful when in full bloom. The leaves are opposite, oval-shaped and 3-5 inches long. During the color season, they turn a rich beautiful scarlet.

The wood of the Dogwood is highly desirable and so valuable that, in many cases, the trees are being harvested for the wood, thus robbing the countryside of their extraordinary beauty. The Dogwood is a very delicate tree and does not stand up well to broken branches and bloom stripping. Many feel that this tree, which is so representative of the south, should be better protected and treated with more respect. The tree is a slow grower and we need to take care of those which are abundant now but may not be so in the future.

Photo 2-37: The exquisite flower of the Dogwood

Photo 2-38: Spring blossoms

Photo 2-39: Fall leaf color

61

SMOOTH SUMAC
Rhus glabra

The Smooth Sumac is more commonly a shrub rather than a tree. However, it produces some of the most beautiful bright, red color to be found in the mountains. There are various kinds of Sumac, among which is a poisonous variety. Fortunately, the poisonous variety is not too common to our region. Two things readily identify the Smooth Sumac. First, the leaves are smooth with finely-toothed edges. They are of the pinnate type (many and parallel on one stem). The Staghorn Sumac has a hairy or velvety covering on the twigs, stem and leaves. Secondly, the Smooth Sumac is accompanied by bright, red berries, as opposed to the white berries of the Poisonous Sumac. Poisonous Sumac is to be avoided at all costs, since it is said to be three times as poisonous as Poison Ivy.

Photo 2-40: The bright leaves of the Smooth Sumac

Photo 2-41: The Smooth Sumac is more a shrub than a tree

GREEN - A COLOR UNTO ITSELF

One of the ingredients which adds to the beautiful fall colors in the mountains is the mixture of green with the changing colors of the leaves.

This green comes primarily from four sources: various Pines, American Holly, Rosebay (known commonly as Rhododendron) and Mountain Laurel. These color sources, which remain green year-round, add much beauty to the fall season and lift our spirits with their splashes of color during the winter months. Not to mention the beautiful clusters of large flowers on the Rhododendron in the spring and the bright, red berries of the American Holly which appear in the fall and persist well into the winter.

Photo 2-42: Green

AMERICAN HOLLY
Ilex opaca

Compared to the English version of the Holly, the leaves of the American Holly are rather dull. The Holly tree can grow as tall as 60 feet, but most often in the south, it rarely exceeds 30 feet with a trunk diameter of 12 inches or less.

The unequal shaped Holly leaves are simple, alternate and exhibit wavy margins with spiny teeth. The leaves remain on the tree for 3 years and then fall off in the spring. The trees are male and female with only the female able to bear the bright, red berries.

The bark of the tree is very light, almost white and normally has wart-like protrusions. The wood of the tree is almost white and is widely used for cabinet work.

Photo 2-43: The contrasting red and green of the American Holly

Photo 2-44: The Holly tree rarely grows this tall in the mountain region

ROSEBAY
Rhododendron maximum

Rosebay, known more commonly as Rhododendron, is a shrub, containing very attractive evergreen leaves. The foliage becomes very thick and can grow to heights up to 25 feet. The beautiful blooming flowers of the springtime (June) range in color from rose to white, making a spectacular mountainous picture.

The evergreen leaves are thick and glossy with a healthy look to them. They are borne in clusters near the end of the twig. They are narrow and oblong and taper at each end. The margins are complete.

The bark of this plant is reddish-brown and is very thin and broken on the surface. Even though Rhododendron has been cultivated into many varieties and is common in gardens and parks, the beauty and setting of the wild Rhododendron is unsurpassed.

Photo 2-45: The Rhododendron leaves (left) are similar but larger than the Mountain Laurel

Photo 2-46: A blooming Rhododendron

MOUNTAIN LAUREL
Kalmia latifolia

The flowers of the Mountain Laurel grow in pinkish-white clusters, are four or five inches across and grow at the end of the twig. As many as seventy-five flowers may exist on a single branch.

Mountain Laural grows as a small tree in our region, sometimes as high as 40 feet. The trunk is short and twisted in appearance. It has simple, dark-green, alternate leaves which are oblong in shape and in general resemble the Rhododendron. The leaves are 2-4 inches long and 1 to 1-1/2 inches wide. The leaves begin to fall during their second summer.

*Photo 2-47: A close-up of the pinkish-white flower
of the Mountain Laurel*

Photo 2-48: The Mountain Laurel in bloom

WHITE PINE
Pinus strobus

Although essentially a northern tree, the White Pine is the most common pine on the mountainous slopes in our region. The tree grows tall (over 100 feet in some instances) and straight. The branches are horizontal with a slight upward turn at the ends.

The needles of the pine are distinct in that they grow in clusters of 5, the only pine to do so. In addition, the cones which mature every two years grow long and slender with a slight curve to them.

The White Pine is a valuable timber tree. It's soft, light wood is adaptable to many uses for general construction work and cabinet making. The tree is a fast grower and is utilized often as a shade and ornamental tree.

Photo 2-49: Taken at Newfound Gap

CHAPTER III
PHOTOGRAPHY TIPS

Autumn is without a doubt the most photographed season in the Appalachian Mountains - and with good reason. It is nature at its most brilliant, with an almost infinite range of colors, from subtle lavenders to vibrant reds, oranges and yellows. This color display almost demands to be photographed. Indeed it is, for it is a rare sight to see a "leaf-looker" without some sort of camera trying to capture on film or video tape the splendor around him. Often, however, the finished photograph doesn't do justice to the original scene. Obviously, an image on a 4" x 6" piece of paper cannot equal the visual impact of viewing layer upon layer of mountain ridges and valleys stretching to the horizon or the feeling of being engulfed in color when standing under the canopy of a maple forest at the peak of color change, but it is possible to record images which are exciting and rewarding. While this chapter is not intended to be a complete guide to outdoor photography (there are many excellent books on that subject), it will offer a few suggestions which might increase your chances of success.

Ideal For Looking

Most people would consider a crisp, cool autumn day with clear, blue skies and bright sunlight to be the ideal day for "leaf looking". In some ways it is, for such a day is perfect for outdoor activities, especially in a place as beautiful as these mountains are at this time of year. But, from a photographic standpoint, it is far from ideal. The harsh, point-source of light created by bright sunlight produces a color-robbing glare on the foliage which can bleach out much of the color resulting in a dull photograph. As this sunlight passes through the trees, an extreme contrast range is created between the deep shadows where the sunlight is blocked by the leaves and the "hot-spots" where the sun passes through. The human eye can cope with this contrast range much better than photographic material. A photograph taken under these conditions would lose detail in both the highlights and the shadows.

Ideal For Photography

A dreary, overcast or rainy autumn day may seem best suited for curling up in front of a fireplace with a good book, but these are precisely the conditions which often offer the photographer the best opportunity for a successful picture. The diffused light of an overcast sky reveals the subtle hues and deep, rich color of the autumn leaves. An early morning fog or a light mist can offer a soft contrast to the vibrant reds and yellows of Maples as well as darkening the trunks of trees which enhances the colors even more. This type of lighting is best suited to the more intimate photographs of individual trees or branches or even close-ups of single leaves. Avoid including the sky in these scenes as it will be a dull gray. (Photo 3-1)

The most dramatic shots of panoramic vistas can often be made under unusual lighting conditions. Such as, after a thunderstorm when the clouds are breaking up and shafts of light are illuminating isolated portions of the mountains.

Photo 3-1: Avoid including the sky on overcast days

Early And Late For Best Results

What if these conditions don't exist or the photographer is unwilling to subject himself or his equipment to the dampness of wet, overcast days? Try getting an early start. The photographer who ventures out before daylight is often rewarded by a brilliant sunrise which may last only a few minutes but will be missed by a less ambitious "leaf-looker". Another fleeting atmospheric occurrence that is often found after a warm day, followed by a cool night, is a low-lying mist or fog which hovers inches above lakes or streams or open meadows. The warm light of the early morning sun can sometimes create a golden glow to this mist which can afford a dramatic backdrop to photographs made through overhanging branches. (Photo 3-2)

An even less common weather condition which can be found only in the early morning hours is a blanket of frost in the low-lying areas. This requires the right combination of humidity, temperature and lack of wind. It also requires a considerable amount of luck (or preparation) on the photographers part to be in the right place at the right time. What might otherwise be an uninteresting subject may be transformed into something spectacular at the moment when the light of the rising sun sparkles off the ice crystals which make up frost. A single leaf or blade of grass or dying fern with its edges rimmed with frost can lead to a very special photograph.

As with the early morning, the light of the late evening hours is much more photogenic than the glaring light of mid-day. As the sun sinks lower on the horizon, the light becomes much "warmer" adding an orange tint to photographs. Also, because this light is less intense, it is possible to photograph directly into the light as it comes through the leaves. This "back-lighting", especially when combined with a background which is in the shade, can give leaves a translucent quality and make them appear as if they have a built-in light source. This same technique can also be used with the slanting light of early morning (Photo 3-3).

Photo 3-2: A light mist serves as a contrast to the vivid colors

Photo 3-3: The evening light produces a back-lighting effect

Filter Out The Bright Light

Even though early mornings or late evenings or overcast, dreary days might offer the best photo opportunities, the average "leaf-looker" will probably spend most of his time enjoying the warmth and sunshine of mid-day. There is one piece of equipment which can dramatically improve the quality of photographs taken under these conditions. That is the polarizing filter. This filter has the ability to block out the polarized light which results from reflections, thus removing much of the glare which robs the leaves of their true colors. The degree of the effect of the filter varies with the angle of the light source to you - being at its greatest when the light is coming from 90 degrees to you and can also be controlled by rotating the filter to create the desired amount of polarization. This filter also has the effect of darkening the sky to a deeper blue, although at its extreme, it might appear unnatural. A polarizing filter might improve any picture under any lighting conditions and it is a simple matter for the photographer to hold the filter up to his eye and rotate it to get an idea of the effect it might have on the photograph (See Photos 3-4 and 3-5).

Another filter, which can help the photo appear more like the original scene, is a warming filter. Photos taken under open shade or on overcast days might appear to be "cool" or have a slightly bluish tint. The amber-tinted 81B (or more strongly tinted 81C) warming filters can correct the colors to a more pleasing and natural color.

Photo 3-4: Not polarized

Photo 3-5: Polarized

79

Tripod And Fast Film

Another piece of equipment that is essential for "serious" photography is a good tripod and cable release. One common element in the "ideal" lighting conditions mentioned earlier is that the amount of light reaching the film is reduced from that available on bright, sunny days. Even those photos taken in bright sun with a polarizing filter will have the light reduced by as much as a factor of four below unfiltered light. There are three basic ways to compensate for this lack of light. One way is to use a "faster" film, that is, one with a higher ISO number. Modern film technology has improved to the point that fast films (those with ISO ratings greater than 200) offer very acceptable color saturation and sharpness. But a rule of thumb, that still holds true, is the slower the film, the sharper the image and the more rich and vibrant the colors will be. Some of the best films available for this type of photography have ISO ratings of 50 or 64. Another way to allow more light to reach the film is to "open up" the lens to a larger lens opening. By doing this, the range of the subject that is in focus, from a point near the camera to a point far away (the "depth of field"), is greatly reduced. This will result in objects near the camera and those far away, being blurred in the final print. While this is sometimes desirable for special effects, it very often is not.

The third technique to achieve proper exposure under low light conditions, is to lower the shutter speed, allowing the light more time to reach the film. Most modern cameras have an automatic mode which adjusts the lens opening or shutter speed automatically to achieve proper exposure. While this is convenient, it may result in a photo with a very narrow "depth of field" or with a blurred image resulting in camera movement during a long exposure. In order to have the most creative control, the photographer must have the ability to choose the lens opening and shutter speed, which gives the desired results. In these low-level lighting conditions, a shutter speed slower than 1/60 seconds is often required. At these shutter speeds, it is virtually impossible to hand-hold a camera and to achieve a critically sharp image. While this may not be immediately apparent in a 3-1/2 by 5 enlargement, any enlargement greater than this will display a noticeable loss of sharpness. Therefore, any advantage in sharpness that might be gained by using a lower speed, fine-grain film will be lost without using a tripod. Also, many people will pay a premium price for a high quality, ultra-sharp lens, only to lose that sharpness by attempting to hand-hold the camera.

There are other reasons for using a tripod. One of the features of the Appalachian Mountains, which adds to their beauty, is the abundance of clear, cascading streams and rivers and countless waterfalls. Classically beautiful photographs of these streams and waterfalls, can be made by allowing the water to blur to a smooth, soft, white streak (Photo 3-6). This requires a very slow shutter speed of less than 1/4 second to several seconds. In order for the other elements of the scene to remain sharp at these shutter speeds, it is essential to firmly support the camera. A good quality, sturdy tripod is the best way to do this.

Photo 3-6: Capture the beauty of water using
slow shutter speed and a tripod

There may be another reason to use a tripod, which is not entirely photographic. Many people find themselves in the mountains during the peak of color change in a long line of traffic, rushing to see what's around the next curve or what the view from the next scenic overlook is like. A typical photograph might be a couple of snapshots taken at an overlook along the Blue Ridge Parkway or the Great Smoky Mountains Parkway before jumping back into the car to reclaim their place in line. The simple act of using a tripod, if nothing else, requires the photographer to slow down. Setting up a tripod, mounting the camera and selecting a spot to place the tripod, takes time and allows the photographer to study the scene more closely. In doing this, he may gain a deeper appreciation of the beauty around him. Once the photographer begins to slow down, he may make more deliberate decisions concerning lens choice, filters, exposure, composition and point of view. After going to the trouble of setting up all these elements, he is more likely to "bracket" the exposure. That is, taking additional shots of the same scene which are over and under the indicated exposure setting in order to insure a properly exposed shot.

Scenes to Remember

Perhaps the primary reason the average person takes a photograph, is to have a record or a reminder of the experience or to have something to show others who were not there. The more successful the photograph is, the less likely it is to be filed away and forgotten. Hopefully, some of the suggestions given will improve your chances of that success. By taking advantage of the right lighting, using film capable of recording the richness of the color and mounting the camera on a sturdy tripod, you will achieve a technically better photograph. But more importantly, take time to "see" the image you are trying to capture. Open up all your senses and enjoy what you are about to photograph. After all, that's what "leaf-looking" is all about - the enjoyment of nature. And, if you are lucky, perhaps the images that you record, will give you enjoyment for years to come.

Photo 3-7: Claydon, Ga., from Black Rock Mountain State Park

Photo 3-8: Cullasaja River - between Highlands, N.C. and Franklin, N.C.

Photo 3-9: River - Smoky Mountain Parkway

84

Photo 3-10: Webb overlook - Smoky Mountain Parkway

Photo 3-11: Chapel - Sky Valley, Ga.

Photo 3-12: Scene from Cullasaja River

Photo 3-13: Snow covered mountain Chimney Tops Trailhead

Photo 3-14: Tiger Mountain, Ga.

Photo 3-15: Cades Cove, Tenn.

Photo 3-16: Horse Cove – Highlands, N.C.

Photo 3-17: Lake Sequoia – Highlands, N.C.

Photo 3-18: Bridal Veil Falls – Highlands, N.C.

GLOSSARY

Acorn— the fruit of the Oaks, consisting of a nut partly enclosed by a scaly cup.

Alternate—leaves, branches or buds which are randomly scattered, singly on the stem, not opposite each other.

Aphyllus— having no leaves.

Apex— the very top, opposite the stem.

Bark— the outer covering of trunks or branches and other shrubs.

Base— the bottom of the blade or leaf.

Bifid— divided in two, longitudinally.

Bipinnate— a compound leaf whose mid-rib is divided into secondary parts which bear the leaflets.

Branch— a secondary division of a tree trunk.

Broadleafs— denotes all trees which have a relatively broad leaf blade as opposed to those with needle-like leaves.

Chlorophyll— the green coloring in plants.

Compound leaf— a leaf which is divided into several similar parts.

Conifer— a cone bearing tree.

Continuous— not interrupted with spaces.

Deciduous— that which is not persistent. Sheds all leaves each year.

Dioecious— bearing male and female flowers on separate plants.

Doubly toothed (senate)— a margin with large teeth which in turn has smaller teeth.

Elliptical— oblong with rounded ends.

Elongated— much longer than broad.

Endemic— peculiar to a small area or region.

Entire— without divisions, lobes or teeth.

Evergreen— remaining green during the winter season.

Foliage— the total of the leaves.

Habitat— the place where a tree grows naturally.

Kernel- the edible part of the nut.

Lance-shaped— elongate in shape, gradually narrowing toward
the lip.

Lateral veins— the side veins of a leaf.

Leaf— the green expansions from the branch of a tree or shrub.

Lobe— a more or less rounded division of an organ.

Midrib— the central vein of a leaf.

Needle— a narrow leaf of such trees as the pines.

Oblong— longer than broad with symmetrical diameters.

Obovate— shape of an inverted egg.

Opposite—leaves, branches or buds which appear directly opposite
each other on the stem.

Oval— broadly elliptical.

Palmate— radiantly lobed or compounded.

Petiole— the stalk of a leaf.

Serrate— toothed: sharp teeth pointing forward.

Shrub— a low plant which commonly divides close to the ground
into many stems.

Tannin— a brown compound found in leaves and bark, used to tan leather.

Terminal— formed at the end; the last.

Trunk— the main stem of a tree.

Veins— the strands of fibrovascular tissue in a leaf.

APPENDIX B
MAIL ORDER INFORMATION

Copies of any pictures appearing in this book (suitable for
aming) may be ordered from Mountain Splendor Publications.
dditional copies of this book may also be ordered.

For ordering information, send a postcard with the words
rder information request" and your return address, to:

Mountain Splendor Publications
P.O. Box 227
Dillard, GA 30537